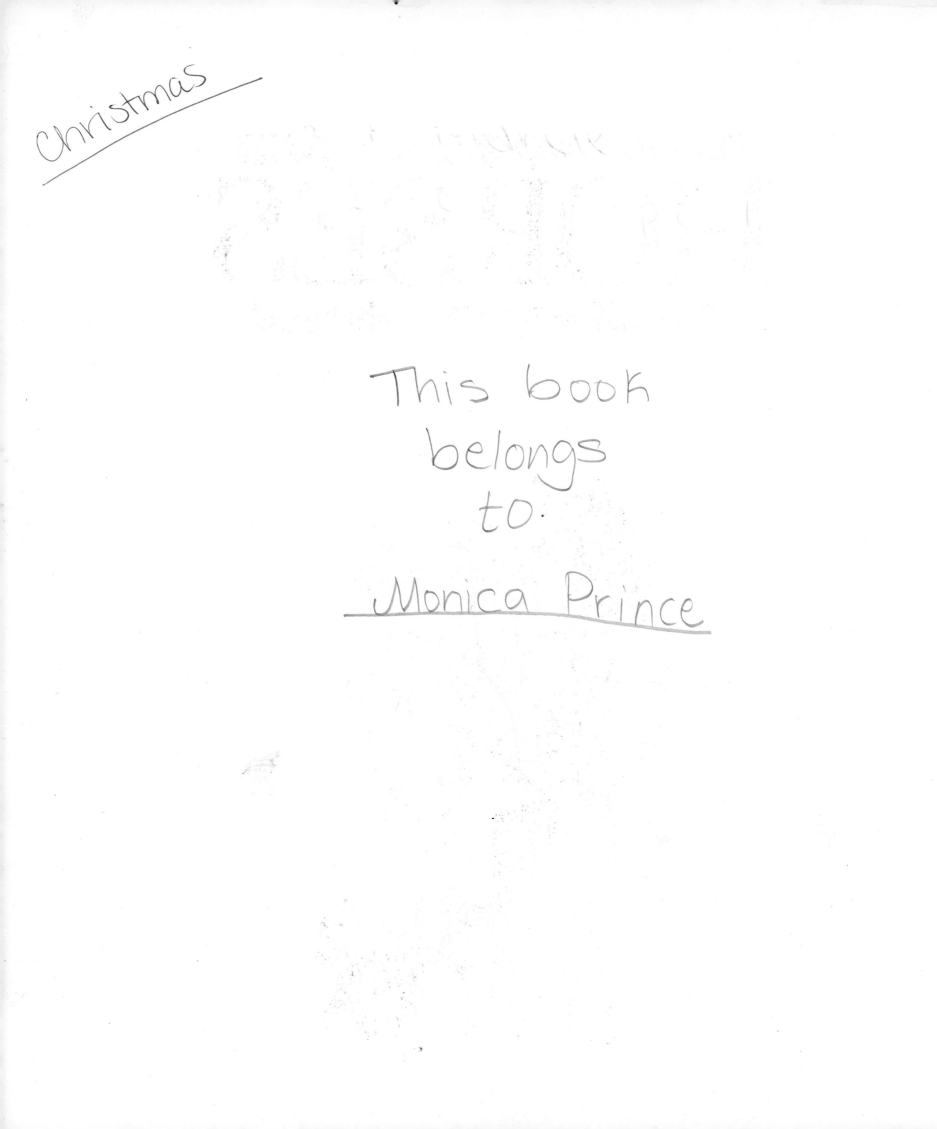

Christmas

This book
belongs
to.

Monica Prince

The *complete book of*
HORSES

JAMES KERSWELL

To: Monica

From: Robbert + Marcie

Given to me as a Christmas present.

To: Monica

The complete book of
HORSES

JAMES KERSWELL

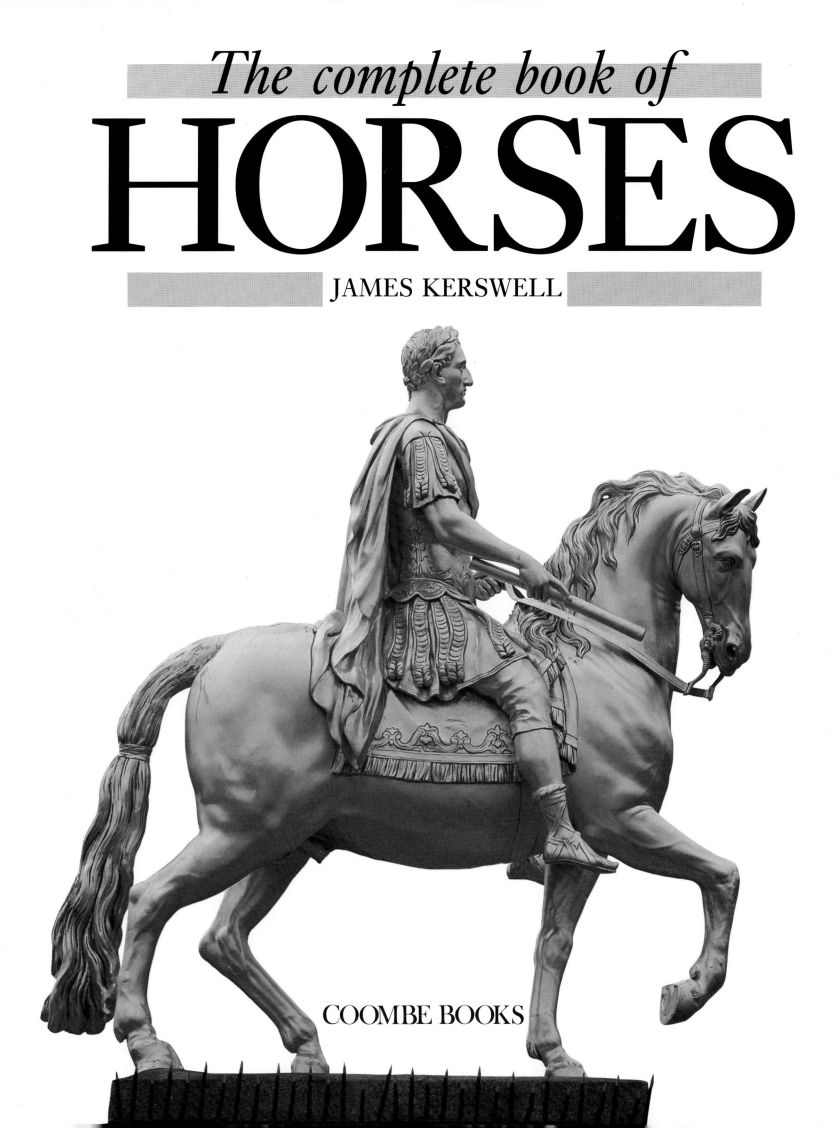

COOMBE BOOKS

CLB 2756
This 1993 edition published by Coombe Books
© 1993 Colour Library Books Ltd, Godalming, Surrey, England
Printed and bound in Hong Kong
ISBN 0 86283 977 7

The Author

James Kerswell grew up surrounded by horses and began his working career as a groom at a stud and livery stables. His experience encompasses not only the specialized care and exercise of quality thoroughbreds, but also a great love of riding, mostly cross country. He is currently employed in forestry near the English/Welsh borders, where he also finds time to teach at his local further education center.

Credits

Edited and designed: Ideas into Print, Vera Rogers and
  Stuart Watkinson
Photographs: Bob Langrish   Layouts: Sue Cook
Typesetting: Ideas into Print
Commissioning Editor: Andrew Preston
Production: Ruth Arthur, Sally Connolly, Andrew Whitelaw
Director of Production: Gerald Hughes
Color Separations: Advance Laser Graphic Arts
  (International) Ltd., Hong Kong.

Above: Modern-day cowboys in Nevada, complete with mobile phones, take a break after rounding up wild Mustangs from the desert. Some of the horses will be adopted as companions or riding horses, thus reducing the wild stock and helping the remainder to survive in their difficult habitat.

Endpapers: Proud heads of two heavy horses - the Brabant, or Belgian draft, and English Shire.

Half-title page: Washing the feet of a patient Clydesdale horse.

Title page: A Roman emperor and his steed in statuesque harmony.

Contents

The horse in history

Like all living creatures, the horse has evolved over a long period of time. It is believed to have existed some 50 million years ago, although it did not resemble modern horses at all, either in size or features. It was about 12in(30cm) tall and looked more like a member of the dog family, especially since at that time it had several toes. However, studies of its fossilized bones have revealed that it was a member of the horse family, and from these remains the experts have been able to pinpoint its place in history quite accurately, identifying it as the earliest form of horse, *Hyracotherium*, more commonly called *Eohippus*. From these fossils it has been possible to build up a fairly accurate description of the movements of these horses, establishing where they originated, where they moved to, what type they were and how much they changed in body structure over the centuries. It is fairly certain that their body types adapted in response to the prevailing climatic conditions and whether these produced lush vegetation or sparse growth. In poorer and more hostile areas where the early horses settled, they evolved into what was to become the finer-boned and faster type of horse.

These horses needed to cover larger areas more quickly and had to be able to escape danger at speed on the open plains. Where the vegetation was richer, the evolving horses had a better diet and more effective cover that provided better protection and reduced the need to run long distances in search of food. These horses grew into the bigger types. As the early horses evolved

Above: *A Roman mosaic depicting a charioteer and his horse. Like the riders in races today, he wore clothing that was colored to represent his sponsor. A leather helmet protected him from the whips of other riders.*

Right: *A statue of the Roman emperor Marcus Aurelius (lived 121-180AD). Horses were important because they raised the general above his troops and enabled him to cover the battlefield at speed when carrying out an inspection.*

Left: *The appearance of Przewalski's horse has remained virtually unaltered for centuries. It is believed to be extinct in the wild, but a long-term breeding plan is in hand to return it to the wild.*

along different routes, several quite distinctive forms gradually developed. The Forest Tarpan, for example, is a small thickset type that was common in the forest regions of Europe until the Middle Ages; the Steppe Tarpan, a bigger and stronger animal, survived until the nineteenth century, but is now extinct in its original form. The only genuine wild horse still in existence that remains the same as its ancient ancestors is Przewalski's horse, which was last seen in the wild in the mountainous regions of the Gobi Desert. The horse played an important part in the lives of our ancient ancestors and helped to change and shape how mankind lived and worked until the beginning of the twentieth century. From the earliest cave drawings as well as statuettes, paintings and

Below: A painting on a pot from the Geometric period, 800BC. It is housed in the Argos Museum in Greece near the site where it was found. Although the picture clearly depicts a horse, the artist has slightly exaggerated its features.

pottery dating back to ancient civilizations in Egypt, Rome and China, we know that the horse has been a beast of burden, the farmer's friend and the warrior's mount. Nor has the horse's sporting potential been overlooked. Many of today's races and events remain little changed from the days when the Romans placed a wager on the local chariot race or Japanese warriors tested their horseback archery skills. Careful breeding and cross-breeding have refined and altered the horse throughout history - from the medieval heavyweights developed to carry a knight in full armor into battle, to today's highly spirited and swiftly elegant racehorses.

Left: Jousting today is a spectacle that takes place purely for the fun and entertainment of both the participants and spectators. It is usually linked with some other form of mock battle event or historical spectacle. Years ago, it was deadly serious, with knights in armor sometimes fighting to the death.

Right: North American Indian warriors prized horses very highly, and painted themselves triumphantly fighting the enemy in battle on their beautiful shields. The riders had to be very skilled in controlling their horses, enabling them to ride at full gallop and shoot arrows without losing balance.

Markings and physique

When you decide to buy a horse or pony, there are two main points to consider: color and physique. Of the two, physique is the most important. A horse's build and general physical condition will tell you much about its qualities and performance and what kind of ride it will be. Naturally, size is important when considering the age and strength of the prospective rider. A good strategy is to scrutinize the horse from a few feet away and mentally divide the body into three: the head, neck and shoulders in one part; the back, ribs and belly in another; and finally the hindquarters and tail. Each part should be well balanced and sound; the head should be well shaped with a good muscular neck that is neither too long nor too short; the eyes clear and bold looking; the muzzle wide but firm; the ears not too long but alert - they should prick forwards when they hear an unfamiliar or sudden noise. Shoulders and legs should be well balanced, with no prominent bones showing from under the skin. The back should be smooth and rise slightly up to the

croup (rump), the chest wide, with plenty of space between the withers (shoulder) and girth groove to accommodate good lungs and a strong heart. Look for a tail carried high on the rump and strong, firm hindquarters and thighs. Legs and feet must be well matched and balanced with the rest of the body, so that the animal is sure-footed when it is led or ridden.

Markings differ from one horse to another, but usually fit into specific categories. The head can have several different marks on it. For example, a spot of white between the eyes is known as a 'star'; if it runs down the face in a narrow line it is known as a 'stripe'; a wider band is known as a 'blaze', but if the face is completely covered in white, the horse is called a 'white face'. These markings are always more striking on a darker horse. The terms used to describe the white markings on the legs of the horse are easily explained. For instance, 'socks' describes the white markings between the bottom of the foot up to - or just above - the fetlock. If the marking continues up towards the knee or beyond, the horse is described as a 'white leg'. The beautiful Pintos, known either as piebalds (black-and-white) or skewbalds (brown-and-white) were especially popular among the North American Indian tribes. These horses are sometimes called the paint horse, because they look as if they have been splashed with paint.

Today, after generations of breeding, there are countless variations in horses' coat shade and color. The choice runs from black through many shades of bay to white, and your final selection is purely a matter of personal preference. The color of a horse has no bearing on its temperament or performance.

Left: *The Percheron is a huge and powerful breed. Here, the horse's mane is neatly combed and the coat has a brilliant sheen.*

Right: *The Appaloosa's markings vary from leopardlike spots to a larger blanket undercolor with spots on the top.*

Points of the horse

Crest Mane Poll
Forelock
Croup Loins Withers Face
Dock
Cheek Muzzle
Throat Chin groove
Flank Shoulder
Hamstring Breast
Sheath
Gaskin Point of elbow
Chestnut Forearm
Hock
Wall of hoof Wrist
Cannon
Ergot Fetlock Pastern
Bulb of heel Hoof
Hollow of heel

Above: An Anglo-Arab horse. Its black mane, tail and stockings are a striking contrast against the bay body color. On the head is a star leading into a stripe. This fine breed of horse has been developed by cross-breeding English Thoroughbreds with Arabs. The parts of the body are labeled using the recognized terminology. The traditional unit for quoting the height of horses is the 'hand' – literally the breadth of the human palm (equivalent to 4in/10.2cm) – a quick and convenient way to judge the animal's height in the absence of any standardized measure.

Color terms applied to horses

A number of color terms have particular meanings when applied to horses:

Bay: Basically brown in various shades from yellow to red, but not dark brown. The points - extremities such as mane and tail - are black.
Brown: Dark brown to almost black. Brown to black points.
Chestnut: Shades from bright golden to the color of cooked liver. Mane and tail same color or paler.
Claybank: A dull brownish yellow - from the color of a bank of clay. Mane and tail slightly darker.
Dun: Literally means a dusty grayish brown, but is applied to various shades from the almost lemon-colored yellow dun to the mouse-colored blue dun. Points are normally black.

Gray: Black and white hairs on a black skin. Shades vary in intensity from light to dark, as well as variations such as flea-bitten gray (light gray speckled with reddish or brown hairs) and dapple gray (darker markings against a light gray background).
Palomino: Golden body with dark eyes and white mane and tail.
Piebald: Patches of black and white. Also known as pinto, in which case it includes the skewbald variation mentioned below.
Roan: White hairs with another color. Variations include blue roan, which is basically black or brown with a dusting of white, and strawberry roan, which is chestnut mixed with white.
Skewbald: Patches of white and any other color except black. Usually refers to brown and white markings.

Right: A chestnut-colored Arab stallion. These horses are renowned for their speed, stamina, gentleness and good looks, all of which make them very popular in the horse world for mixing and cross-breeding with other horses.

Below: A herd of Akhal-Teke grazing on scrubland in Russia. They are not very large horses - only about 15 hands high - but hardy and rather high-spirited. The colors are usually dun, gray or bay and the coat has a shiny appearance to it.

Above: The Pinto may also be called the paint horse, obviously because of its stunning color markings. The name Pinto describes the horse's color and can apply to any horse or pony, because it is not a breed in its own right. (The golden-colored Palomino is also sometimes mistakenly thought to be a breed.) There are two types of Pinto-colored horses. This one is brown-and-white and known as skewbald. The other one is black-and-white and described as piebald. Some breeds of birds, such as the budgerigar or magpie, are also identified by the same name. At fancy dress events, the Pintos can be quite eye-catching and their colors can become an integral part of the costume, as well as distracting attention from any mistakes made by the rider!

Left: The beautiful and elegant Andalusian horse is renowned for its fine movements and is another breed favored by the famous Spanish Riding School in Vienna. There it performs one particular movement known as the Capriole: the horse jumps up from a standstill and kicks outwards in a striking action.

Right: An absolutely splendid example of a French Percheron. They are either black or gray in color and do not have as many feathers on the fetlocks as other heavy horse breeds. As you can see, this particular horse is in excellent condition. With its large muscular hindquarters and strong-looking shoulders, it is no wonder that it was once very popular among the farming communities for all the heavy pulling work, for shunting implements around the farm and operating them out on the land. Now that such animals are no longer needed for agricultural labor, their appearance is restricted to specialist shows and displays around the world. It is sad to think that nowadays such horses are generally bred for the quality of their meat.

Left: Two Standardbred foals. One day they will be fast and furious on the race track, where this breed is famous for trotting. These horses resemble the Thoroughbred in looks.

Below: The lively Breton is a good-tempered, thickset breed that makes a good, stocky draft horse. Despite being muscular, it is not particularly tall, standing around 14.3 to 16 hands tall. Most Bretons are red roan colored, but there are also chestnuts, grays and blue roans.

Right: The proud stance of a Saddlehorse, with its classic skewbald pinto markings, is typical of the exuberant style of the American plantation horse. They enjoy a great popularity in the southeastern states. The splashed markings on a mainly white coat are sometimes called Tobiano.

Left: *A meager desert diet, harsh conditions and inbreeding to maintain purity of type do not seem to have impaired the excellent physique of today's purebred Arab. In fact, more recent strains of Arab developed in European and North American studs have tended to produce a softer, less lean-looking horse. The small, but hardy and resilient Arabs were once the prized possessions of Bedouin tribesmen. Today they are the cornerstone of most quality saddlebreeds in the Western world. Three main types of Arab horse can trace their origins back to those fine Bedouin mounts: the Muniqi tends to be lean and rangy, built for speed; the more muscular Kehylan has great stamina and strength; while the more delicate Seglawui is famed for its elegant and rather graceful build.*

Above: *The American wild Mustang, also sometimes called the Cayuse or, more commonly, the Bronco. These were the first cow ponies to be used for herding stock on the plains. These days, they are more often seen in the rodeo arena, where their tendency to throw and buck their rider tests the skill of the cowboys and other riders willing to chance their luck. Not all riders can stay on the Bronco's back until the buzzer sounds, as the horse is very strong and fierce and soon throws them off. Sadly, apart from the rodeos that keep the breed going, the number of wild Mustangs has drastically diminished. Over the years, the horses have been hunted and shot down because of the damage they did to much of the best pastureland required for controlled grazing. Many were also shot as a good source of cheap dog food.*

Left: The stunning color and physique of this golden Palomino is quite outstanding. The tail has been carefully brushed and left as long as possible; the mane and forelock have also been brushed neatly to emphasize the golden color even more. This particular horse has obviously caught the judge's eye for its superior looks and good grooming.

Below: A nicely shaped head and a broad but firm muzzle make for a good-looking horse. Its healthy eyes are large and round, clear sighted and clean; the ears inquisitively alert and pointing forwards. Instead of straggling over the face, the mane and forelock are neatly plaited and this helps to show off the horse's fine face.

Left: This chestnut horse has a 'white face', a marking that covers almost the whole face and muzzle. A thin white line down the face is a 'stripe' and a 'star' is a white mark on the forehead between the eyes. A 'snip' is a white mark on either the left or righthand side of the nostril.

Life cycle of the horse

Horses that live in the wild mate in the spring, which ensures that, as long as the pregnancy runs its full term, the harsh winter weather will have passed and there will be plenty of fresh grass for the mother and new foal to eat in the following spring. The horse's natural sex drive is controlled accordingly. An increase in libido at the right time is caused by a hormone called FSH (follicle stimulating hormone), which is released from a pituitary gland just below the brain. A combination of factors triggers the release of FSH, including the increased hours of daylight as summer approaches and light is absorbed through the eyes and passed to the brain; warmer atmospheric conditions, and increased protein levels from the new lush grasses. The FSH travels through the horse's bloodstream to the ovaries, where it causes the minute eggs to grow. Soon after this another hormone called LH (luteinizing hormone) is released, which causes the enlarged egg to release itself from the ovary. If the mare is serviced by the stallion at this stage of ovulation and everything is normal, the mare will conceive.

Mares generally ovulate every 22 days or so and could, therefore, become pregnant at any time of the year. However, the chances of this happening are less likely outside the springtime peak period, not just because the mare's ovulation period is less frequent, but also

Above: For the first few days after birth, the mare guards the foal closely, making sure it is familiar with her smell and color.

Right: A group of young Welsh ponies. Even when a foal has befriended other horses, the bond with its mother remains strong.

because the stallion does not produce as much sperm. In order to fit in better with the racing year, certain stud farms have produced good breeding results with thoroughbreds by artificially stimulating the spring hormone activity. This can be done by lighting the stable to prolong daylight hours, heating the horse's living accommodation and by adding high-protein supplements to the feed. Although this method does not produce the same percentage of pregnancies as might be expected in the wild, the success rate is good - somewhere in the region of 70 percent of the normal birthrate.

Twins are unusual in a horse, because the mare's uterus is too small to carry two fetuses to full term and a miscarriage invariably results. Following a gestation period of about 11 months, or approximately 340 days from conception, the mare gives birth, usually unaided. The foal is born forelegs first and should be able to stand after two hours. It soon begins to suckle. If it has not moved after an hour it must be ailing. The mare is very protective of her foal, not allowing anyone or anything near it for several days. It can follow her around the field and eat grass almost immediately, but relies mainly on its mother's milk for the first three months. A foal could be weaned at about six months, by which time it will be reasonably confident in its new surroundings and will have found new friends.

Right: For most horse owners hoping to breed from a good mare, the prospect of keeping their own stallions for the job is simply not practical or affordable. Stud fees vary according to the potential value of the foals. The mare is therefore taken to the stud farm, where the best facilities and professional help are available. The peak time for conception is in the spring, but the mare could conceive at any time, as long as she remains receptive to the stallion (for about five days in each cycle) and producing a special scent to attract him.

Above: Mating at the stud is strictly controlled to ensure the maximum chance of success, as the services of stallions can be very expensive. Heated stalls and a high-protein diet to stimulate hormone production may be part of the service for top-quality horses in an effort to produce a valuable foal.

Right: After showing few signs early on, the mare's belly begins to swell noticeably when she is about seven months pregnant. It is important to make sure that she is given extra food, as well as care and attention throughout the term to help ensure that the newborn foal is born healthy.

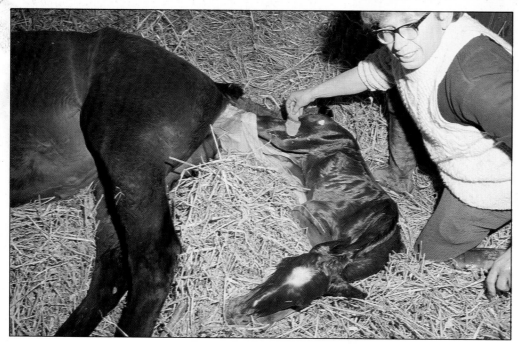

Left: Most foals are born at night and the birth usually lasts about 20 minutes. The mare lies on her side and pushes the foal out forelegs first. These may appear quite soon and you might begin to wonder if the rest will ever follow. This does not always happen quickly and sometimes it takes hours before the mare begins to push hard and deliver the foal. Once the biggest part – the head and shoulders – have been pushed out, the rest of its body will follow easily, and just as soon as she gets her breath back the mare begins to clean the newborn foal.

Right: After struggling continuously almost right from the beginning of birth, the foal can usually stand on its own completely unsupported after two hours. This can be quite an amusing sight if you stand and watch it poke and prod around with its muzzle as it instinctively knows that its mother can provide it with some sort of nourishment. Eventually, it will be rewarded perhaps by its mother encouraging it to find its way to her teats and suckle on the vitally important first milk, or colostrum, which contains vitamins and antibodies.

Left: On many studs, foals are weaned off the mares at six months old. It is true that by this time they have been given a good start nutritionally and are reasonably independent. Also, being valuable domesticated animals, they are likely to be well looked after. Psychologically, however, both mare and foal can find the enforced separation a wrench and may be very unhappy for a while. Under natural conditions in the wild, the mare may continue to suckle the foal for up to three years and enjoy its companionship as they run and rest together. This is not the case should she foal again before that time; as soon as the new foal is born the mare will reject the yearling by repeatedly pushing it away. The young horse usually accepts the situation.

Left: The foal continues to suckle from its mother for about a year, maybe as long as two or three if she does not foal again. It will happily graze beside her in the field and make friends with other foals of the same age after only a few days. But should it find itself on its own, it will utter a shrill, frightened call, which the mother will answer with a deep reassuring rumble.

Right: These Welsh ponies are quite happy in each other's company, even when confined to quarters. For the lone horse, the stable can represent the security it misses with the herd. Insecurity may cause it to bolt for home if frightened by a sudden noise or movement when it is out. A lone horse may also get bored in the stable, which can lead to behavioral problems in future.

Below: *Young foals look comically ungainly and long-legged and it is hard to believe that this inelegant animal will grow into a powerful and handsome thoroughbred. With its short neck and long legs, a foal may have difficulty at first in reaching the ground to graze. Once it starts grazing and suckling less, the foal's growth rate decreases and at one year old it will be about 80 percent of its final height. It is not fully developed until its fifth year - sometimes later - so it is vital not to over-exert a horse in its early years.*

Right: *Lippizaner mares with their foals. These magnificent white horses are extensively bred for the Spanish Riding School in Vienna, where they are rigorously trained for about seven years as performing horses. Intelligent and disciplined, the horses are taught to jump, kick and trot on the spot in set movements. They were first developed in 1580 at the Austrian Archduke's imperial stud in the village of Lippiza (now in Yugoslavia), where breeding continues today.*

Right: Horses can be trained from a very early age. In fact, it is a good idea to introduce gentle but firm handling as soon as the foal can run about, because it will accustom the horse to being led before you tackle more advanced training. It is also important for a young foal that spends a lot of its time indoors to be given some form of exercise, so as soon as it is familiar with being led, take it outdoors and walk or run it around a field or paddock. A head slip will allow you to lead the horse about and control it if necessary. To ensure the foal does not jump and run or get out of control, lead it quite close to the head. This will discourage any naughty pranks, such as rearing or shying, from the very start.

Below: The head slip is useful for tethering as well as exercising the young foal and will make it easier for the animal to cope with a bridle later on. Be sure to fit the head slip properly and adjust it regularly as the horse grows.

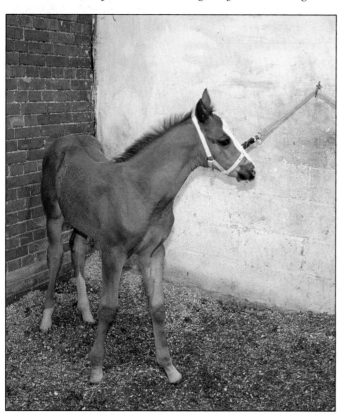

Left: Long before you can begin to ride a young horse, you should spend time exercising it on a lunge rein. Walking – and later running – will harden the muscles and help to strengthen the heart and lungs. Ten minutes is enough to start with, slowly increasing to half-an-hour once the horse is fit. It is important to exercise the horse thoroughly throughout the developmental stage of its life. Avoid using any form of riding equipment at first. Later, you can introduce a saddle and once the young horse is used to having this on its back, you can gradually weight it using, say, small sandbags. Eventually the horse will be confident enough to allow a rider on its back. Nevertheless, the lunging exercises should continue so that the horse keeps to a familiar routine and still gets plenty of exercise.

Above: All horses have a deep-rooted herding instinct and will live more happily together than alone, when they tend to feel fearful and lonely. In the wild, the herd has a dominant mare that leads them to water or grazing and whose authority is never challenged. In return, she is responsible for protecting the others from any danger. This pattern of behavior can be identified in domestic groups of horses too; a strict order of importance ensures that horses rarely fight – a warning nip is usually emough should one member of the group step out of line. Understanding this is a key to controlling a horse; in order to tame and teach a horse successfully, the owner must assume the role of the dominant animal. This is clearly easier with a horse that would normally be low on the herd scale of importance.

All shapes and sizes

If it had not been for the demand for heavy horses in the past - for farmwork and on the battlefield - it is almost certain that most of the large breeds would not exist today. The great French Percheron is a classic example. It is one of the largest horses in the world, but now its controllable strength and power are no longer highly regarded and it is destined principally for the meat markets. The same applies to another French breed, the Boulonnais; what an ignominious end to the career of a breed once used by Napoleon to pull heavy artillery weapons on the battlefield. Most developed countries have their own heavy large horses, principally bred to pull the plow and other labor-saving farm implements, and although their role has been largely superseded by machines, there are still jobs where the horse cannot be bettered. In remote mountain areas, for example, where trucks and tractors could never be transported, mules are the only means of access. In forestry, horses can haul heavy lumber where wheeled motor vehicles cannot go or would not be safe, such as on a dangerous incline. Even in highly developed countries there are communities that prefer a slower pace of life and still farm with horses. Then there are the world's countless miles of waterways; many barges and canal boats are now fitted with engines, but the old barge horse plodding steadily along the towpath is a cleaner, quieter and much more leisurely form of power.

At the other end of the scale are the miraculous miniature horses and the smallest ponies - some so tiny that they can take shelter underneath the heavy horse's haunches. Like their giant cousins, many have been specially bred because their dimunitive size makes them an excellent choice for children. The Falabella, the world's smallest horse, is so tiny it cannot even be ridden, but is bred and kept purely for its novelty value or as a tourist attraction. Slightly larger and hugely popular is the Shetland pony, once a useful working horse in the coal mine and on the farm for pulling trucks and carts, but now one of the best-loved mounts for children. Strong, sturdy and undeniably handsome, the Pony of the Americas is specially bred as a child's horse. With its relatively sleek physique and handsome colored coat, this Shetland cross looks more like a true miniature horse than a pony. In parts of the world where the terrain is bleak and the living is hard, small stocky ponies have been developed as all purpose work horses, hardy and full of stamina, yet requiring little grazing.

Left: Even a pony too small to ride can be very strong, and you can have fun training it to pull a light trap or carriage.

Right: Averaging 17 hands high, the Shire is the largest horse in the world. Once a war horse, it is still famed for its strength.

Above: The Jutland is an ancient breed of Danish draft horse that originated in the Jutland region. It was originally bred in the Middle Ages as a traditional war horse - the kind intended to carry heavily armored knights into battle. Despite its warlike background, the Jutland, in common with most heavy horses, has a sweet and gentle nature. Usually a dark chestnut color, with a blond mane and tail, the Jutland has a large weighty body with a deep chest and short neck. The feathers at the bottom of its feet are a distinctive feature, being blond to match the horse's mane. When the much nimbler cavalry horse rendered these rather slow-moving breeds obsolete in battle, the Jutland became the most popular breed of farm horse in Denmark, and was eventually crossbred with the English Suffolk Punch to improve its suitability still further.

Right: The Trait du Nord is known for its immense strength, hardiness and eagerness to work. It stands about 16 hands high (which is just over 5ft 4in/ 1.63m at the shoulder) and weighs as much as 2,205lb(1,000kg). This good-natured, heavy draft horse can still be seen working the fields in northern France where it originated. Unfortunately, however, France's heavy horse population has dwindled by some 80 percent in recent years. The Trait du Nord may be chestnut, bay or roan. Its resemblance to the Ardennais - although a little longer - is due to the fact that it is bred from the Ardennais crossed with a Brabant. In fact, it comes from the same region as the Ardennais and is sometimes known as the Ardennais du Nord.

Right: Until the middle of the twentieth century, one in every five horses in Hungary was a Murakoz. This heavy-duty farm horse takes its name from the river Mura in southern Hungary, where it originates, and is a result of crossbreeding with the best Hungarian stallions, Percherons, Nordikers and Ardennais. Spirited but obedient, it became extremely popular as a powerful worker, standing some 16 hands high. Unfortunately, the number of Murakoz horses around the world is dwindling, as people find them too expensive to keep and breed. Displays and exhibitions are the only salvation for these relics of the past.

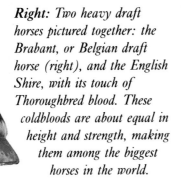

Right: Two heavy draft horses pictured together: the Brabant, or Belgian draft horse (right), and the English Shire, with its touch of Thoroughbred blood. These coldbloods are about equal in height and strength, making them among the biggest horses in the world.

Left: A team of dray horses, neatly turned out for show day and proudly pulling a small dray – a strong cart designed to carry heavy loads. Everyone enjoys the sight of these magnificent creatures in all their finery, tossing their plumes and bells. Fortunately, such events promote continued interest in these large horse breeds, now that they are no longer needed in the fields. What began as a publicity exercise has turned out to make such economic sense that it has enabled some horses to go back to work on a daily basis. Some city breweries have found that a team of drays is the quickest and cheapest way to make local beer deliveries. Otherwise, these massive but lovable animals rely on enthusiasts to feed, exercise and groom them, and to keep all that tack in tiptop condition.

Right: The Suffolk Punch is one of the purest breeds of ancient heavy horse and can be traced back to the 18th century. It comes from East Anglia in the UK, which has a strong farming tradition. It is easy to identify, being a rich chestnut color, with a compact body, short legs and, unusually for a coldblood, no feathers at its heels. Standing just over 16 hands high, the Suffolk is not just a powerful and reliable worker, but also moves well, especially when trotting. Its great strength and peaceful character have made it a very popular choice in the past – although being economical to feed and long lived may also have contributed to its reputation. Unlike the Shire horse, the Suffolk Punch can survive on a relatively small amount of food, considering its great power and size.

Right: In an effort to prevent the disappearance of ancient large breeds, even though they have largely outlived their useful role, a Shire Horse Center has been set up in the UK. Here visitors can see the big horses in action and find out what is involved in caring for them, including feeding, grooming and, as shown here, shoeing them. In fact, there is no immediate danger of the Shire becoming extinct, since these giants of the horse world remain a popular show attraction. Colors vary from black or gray to brown and bay. The face is usually white and there are silky white feathers from the knee downwards. Like all coldbloods – horses with a typically even temperament and heavy physique – the Shire horse is a calm and kindly animal.

Above: Miniature horses are kept mainly for their novelty value, as pets or as a show attraction. Sometimes you also see them in zoos, where their breeding can be professionally monitored and their survival as a breed type is assured. A few of the more sturdy small horses and ponies are strong enough to be ridden and make an ideal first mount for young children, but most are generally too small for the saddle. However, some may be strong enough to pull a scaled-down trap or small cart, perfect for lucky children to learn early horse-driving skills. Miniature horses and ponies come in a wide variety of colors and types and are bred mostly as a hobby, as they have no useful value. They sometimes appeal to those who love horses but who do not have the room or facilities to keep a full-sized animal.

Right: The American Shetland stands slightly taller than the true Scottish Shetland from which it was originally bred - it can reach 46in(115cm) whereas the Shetland is not allowed to exceed 42in(105cm). With the much better grazing and more favorable climate in the USA, it is difficult to keep the size down to the short stature expected of a Shetland, which is accustomed to the harsher conditions of the Scottish islands. However, there is one characteristic of this hardy breed that has been passed on to its American cousins thanks to selective breeding: the pony is tremendously strong, capable of pulling twice its own weight, and a popular contestant in pulling contests. The American Shetlands are also popular racing ponies and have distinguished themselves on the half-mile race track.

Left: *The diminutive Pony of the Americas is one of the world's best documented breeds. It was specially bred in Iowa in the 1950s as a children's pony, the result of cross-breeding an American Shetland stallion with an Appaloosa mare. All the descendants of this union have been Appaloosa colored, with seven pattern variations of spots. This distinctive little horse stands 11.2 to 13 hands high and has a gentle, obedient nature, making it an ideal first mount. Despite its elegant body shape, it has proved unexpectedly strong and sturdy. A handsome if pint-sized breed, the Pony of the Americas looks more like a small-scale version of the Quarter horse crossed with an Arab than a plump pony.*

Left: Records show that the tiny Shetland pony may attain no more than 26in (65cm) in height and yet it has the strength and stamina to carry an adult rider many miles, albeit not in great comfort. Shetlands are lively and intelligent ponies and a popular choice for children because of their size. Their stunted growth is believed to be due to the lack of food and fierce weather conditions on their native islands in the north of Scotland, where they have been known since 500BC. Their hardiness is legendary: in winter their coats grow immensely thick and when food is short they will eat seaweed off the beach. Height is restricted, but all coat colors are allowed, including piebald and skewbald patterns. Dark brown and black are most commonly seen.

Right: The perfectly proportioned Falabella is the world's smallest horse. At less than seven hands high (28in/72cm), it is not large enough to be ridden, but makes a bright, affectionate pet and companion. It was bred in Argentina by crossing a particularly small Shetland mare with a very small Thoroughbred stallion. Most color options are allowed, but Appaloosa markings are the most highly prized.

Below: The Hafflinger pony is a pretty little thing. Although tall for a pony – it stands about 14 hands high – it has an almost dainty appearance. However, this belies a toughness and stamina that have earned it a reputation as a reliable workhorse in its native Austria. Today it is valued as a trekking pony.

Below: Intelligent, muscular, and sure-footed, a small Welsh pony makes a delightful and practical mount for a child. The head has all the nobility of an Arab, the eyes are intelligent and the body is compact and robust. It can be any color except piebald or skewbald, but gray, bay or chestnut are commonly found. Such horses have been bred selectively for centuries, thus ensuring that their best characteristics remain strong.

Bred for a purpose

People have been actively breeding horses for hundreds of years and the practice continues today. Halfbreds are mixed with purebreds, warmbloods with coldbloods and so on, in an effort to create an animal that suits man's needs more exactly. Not all these cross-breedings - or indeed pure-breedings - turn out to be exactly what was desired or expected, and this is what makes the process all the more interesting (and costly). Unfortunately, horse breeding has become a highly commercialized venture; some pure breeds can sell for astronomical sums and fortunes exchange hands with little or no regard for the animal itself. One of the most popular and sizeable groups of horses to have been specially bred are the sporting animals. The horses with the greatest speed and stamina command the highest stakes, and breeders carefully select the horses that win most consistently and are top of their class from which to breed future generations of potential record breakers. Sporting games involving horses are played throughout the world and most countries have a sport billed as the nation's favorite pastime. Such events are often worth a great deal of money to the winning owners, and participating horses are so valuable that only a small minority of people can afford to own or race one. However, in some sports, pleasure and entertainment are equally important and here the attributes of the equine competitors may be less exacting. Specially bred horses

continue to play a leading role in the circus and in traditional shows and displays around the world. They are selected partly for their striking appearance, such as a spotted coat or large muscular body, but even more important is their ability to learn a complicated series of movements and actions that often date back centuries. At one time, the working horse was probably the most important of all the breeds, but today it is at the lower end of the market in terms of price and demand. Once bred for its strength, reliability and versatility, now it is almost an anachronism, except in a few countries where a horse or pony is the only means of practical power. As the demand for these stocky breeds declines, their numbers are kept to a minimum, but the traditional characteristics of horses such as the Shire and Ardennais are carefully preserved lest the breed type be lost. We must hope that shows and parades throughout the world will foster an interest in these old types of horse and that enthusiastic breeders will continue to maintain their existing stocks for the future.

Left: This finely bred French Saddlehorse may make a competition horse for jumping or eventing, a racehorse or a strong mount well suited to riding schools or trail riding.

Right: Horse racing is one of the most popular and important sports in the world. Some of the horses have been bred over many generations by selecting fast and expensive breeds.

Below: *This group of horses has been trained together as a team and now performs as a spectacular circus act. The horses must be able to gallop evenly in a relatively small space - the circus ring is only about 42ft(13m) in diameter - so the legs must be strong and correctly aligned and the horses need plenty of stamina to keep up the pace and carry an adult rider. Shorter legs in the ideal performing breeds makes it easier for the rider to jump on and off.*

Above: *There are several horse schools in the world, such as the famous French cavalry school, the Cadre Noir, where large but agile muscular breeds perform a series of quite awe-inspiring movements, developed over many years to produce a spectacular sequence. They undergo vigorous daily training to keep them in good shape and in peak condition. The horse pictured here has jumped several feet off the ground. It is held by long reins and responds directly to its instructor's commands.*

Above right: *The purebred Arabs are probably the most beautiful and highly coveted horses in the world. They have been crossbred with just about every other type of horse, especially in the racing classes. Alongside the English Thoroughbreds, they are the fastest horses in the world and have the stamina to run long distances carrying a rider. The breed is also known for its high spiritedness - important in a horse destined to enjoy the thrill of the race - and a toughness that belies its elegant appearance.*

Right: *The circus ring is one of the few places where you can see a certain type and breed of horse en masse, and what a beautiful sight they make, especially if they have been chosen not just for their breed characteristics of strength and obedience, but for the closest possible match in height and color too. Here the combination of liver and white is stunning, even without the fancy headdresses and other trappings of the performing horse. Cleverly, the horses know their place in the herd and the two colors are neatly segregated with striking effect.*

Left: The stocky mule, the offspring of a male ass and a female horse, is traditionally a beast of burden, strong and broad enough to carry a heavy load and with the stamina to withstand difficult terrain and long days without nourishment.

Below: The Barb has played a major role in the development of foreign blood lines. It is used in crossbreeding to strengthen other breeds with its sturdy physique and good but high-spirited nature.

Below: As its name implies, the Saddlebred has been particularly developed for its suitability as a good riding horse. Yet most of the horses in this class are excellent all-rounders, competing at show jumping, racing and cross country events, all of which makes them popular show horses. Good-looking and graceful in all its movements, the breed has two extra gaits to produce a smooth and elegant ride: the rack, which is an even, fast prance with the foot pausing in midair; and a high-stepping slow gait. The body is short and muscular with slim, hard legs, and the head is small and alert, with an arched neck. As well as having an enviable physique, the Saddlebred is a good-natured and comfortable ride. The American Saddlebred, or Kentucky Saddler, is usually bay, black, chestnut or gray. Sometimes the elegantly high tail is surgically altered so that it stands up at a steep angle.

Above: The Hungarian Furioso breed is about 150 years old, and still extensively bred as a fine horse for show jumping, eventing, dressage and steeplechasing. Its origins can be traced back to a Thoroughbred imported from the UK, and the breed has been mixed with other Thoroughbreds over the years to give it even finer attributes.

Above: The Andalusian is prized as an excellent riding horse, with intelligence, strength and a proud stature. It stands approximately 16 hands high. Its origins are in Africa, but it has been associated with Spain for many centuries.

Left: Some riding horses are crossbred with a purebred type - either Thoroughbred or Arab - to produce a halfbred, or warmblood, that has the advantage of improved speed and stamina. This type of crossbreeding produces a more nimble and active horse that is easy to train.

Below: Originally, the cavalry horse was intended to offer the best advantage in battle, but several of these breeds survive today on account of their great strength and agility. The cavalry horse was required to perform a complicated series of movements, both in battle and on the parade ground, and to have a temperament that remained unruffled by the surrounding mayhem. These qualities naturally make it a fine performing horse and the breeds are prized by the world's last two remaining academies where these classical movements are still taught: the Spanish Riding School in Vienna and the French Cavalry School in Saumur, where this picture was taken. It takes seven years to train a horse and it must learn to leap vertically from a standstill, to crouch and to rear up.

Right: Because they have a short muscular body and an even temper, ponies are the ideal mount for children. They need to be sure-footed and intelligent to cope with the rigors of a young and inexperienced rider. Most are hardy, coming originally from strong working stock, which also equips them well for their role today as children's pets and playthings. Being small and confident, they also have a new and popular role as a trekking horse, since many breeds are strong enough to carry adult riders for long distances over difficult terrain. There is no specific breeding program for the majority of ponies and many have been crossbred away from their original type. For this reason, some of the ancient moorland ponies are being specially bred in an attempt to preserve their true characteristics.

Right: A good horse for show jumping needs to be fast, well muscled and strong, yet small and agile enough to maneuver difficult obstacles, and able to leap nimbly and accurately over jumps as high as itself. Total concentration is required on the part of both rider and horse if points are not to be lost, and a great deal of practice time is required to build up the necessary level of teamwork. No specific breed is particularly suited to the skill.

Left: The American Quarter horse is one of the oldest and most popular American breeds, with nearly 1,500,000 registered horses in the USA alone. It is favored throughout the world for its powerful body and even temperament, and was originally developed as a smart mount for rich plantation owners. Quarter horse racing is extremely popular, both in Australia and the USA; the big race to compete in is the Futurity Stakes in California, with high stakes. As well as a sporting horse, the Quarter is a fine cattle horse and is much in demand for ranch work.

53

Choosing a horse

Owning a horse involves assuming a variety of responsibilities, as well as anticipating the prospect of fun and enjoyment. First of all you must cater for the horse's needs, which means providing somewhere for it to shelter, either in a purpose-built stable or in a suitable building where the horse can feel contented. It should be equipped with a water supply so that the horse can be watered and washed down, and also have a dry, separate storage space for foodstuffs. Take care not to leave food tubs open and clear up all spillages, as these will soon attract rodents that bring unwanted germs and diseases, which could easily pose a threat to your own health as well as that of the horse. Another essential provision is somewhere for your horse to run about freely without the risk of coming to any harm from bad fencing and carelessly discarded sharp or broken materials. Accidents can lead to unnecessary suffering and costly veterinary bills. Fences can be made of various types of materials, providing they cannot be easily broken and do not have sharp corners and points on which the horse could impale itself. This can happen when an animal runs tightly against a fence – as is often the case. Replacing existing fences can be expensive, so it helps if you can do some or all the work yourself to reduce costs. Remove any broken glass and loose debris and fill any holes that might cause the horse to stumble, injuring or even breaking a limb.

Acquiring clothes and accessories for both horse and rider does not usually cause much of a problem, as there are many shops that specialize in supplying tack, as this equipment is called. There is usually a thriving secondhand market for these goods, so your budget need not be stretched too far, but do check that the equipment you buy is of strong quality and in good condition.

Having satisfied yourself that you have a place to keep your horse and all the equipment, you are ready to start looking for a suitable horse or pony. Ask yourself how good a rider you are and what do you expect from your horse. If you are just starting out with horses and are feeling unsure, invest in some riding lessons and learn how to cope with the different techniques and grooming methods. The size of a suitable horse depends on your height and weight, and whether you will use it for simple country rides or competing in several different strenuous events. If possible, ask someone with specialized knowledge, such as a veterinarian, to examine the horse for you and ask to see any previous records, if available. All this will help you assess whether the horse is the right one for you. Take your time and do not be afraid to ask the owner questions about the animal. Try to get some idea of its temperament and handling qualities. Pet it, talk to it, ride it and, if you are not satisfied, carry on looking until you *have* found the right horse. Once your chosen horse moves in, allow a week or two for it to settle down and always keep to the daily routine it has been used to. Finally, remember that a good affectionate relationship is just as important as these practical points.

Right: Once mutual confidence is won, a horse of your own soon becomes a faithful friend.

Far right: A successful jumper needs patience and care in training over several years. Ideally, a good grounding in dressage will encourage the best handling technique.

Left: *The most suitable kind of horse for dressage is accustomed to human contact as early as possible, even though training does not start in earnest until the horse is between three and five years old. At five years of age its potential for the sport can be more keenly assessed.*

Below: *The tiny Falabella is usually kept as a novelty or pet, especially where the family may love horses but does not have the space or facilities for a full-sized breed. Although it is too small to be ridden, the Falabella still needs care and attention.*

Right: *The American Quarter horse is recognized as the most popular breed in the world. It is gentle and easy to handle, yet powerfully built and strong enough to carry a grown man in race or rodeo. Despite being muscular and fairly massive-looking in the body, the horse's general appearance is one of compact elegance and sleek good looks. This is also an intelligent horse, and a favorite for stock work among cattle ranchers. The Quarter horse was originally bred by plantation owners in Virginia and the Carolinas as a quarter mile sprint racer, with fast acceleration as a prime aim.*

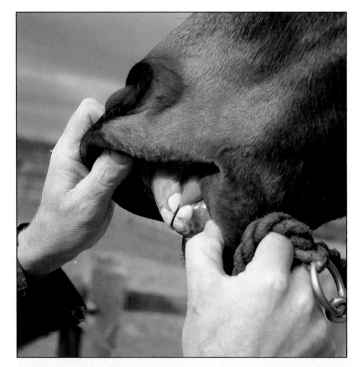

Left: Checking a horse's teeth and the appearance of its mouth can be an indication of age but is not a foolproof method of 'aging' the animal. A horse's teeth grow as they wear down and also lengthen with age. They will not only grow longer but also begin to slope and protrude outwards.

Below: Unless you are really experienced with horses, it is a good idea to have a qualified veterinarian check your potential horse over for you. After a thorough examination, he will be able to tell the horse's general health and if it has any specific weaknesses.

Right: Testing the horse's tendons. A strained tendon is quite common and will be indicated by swelling caused by the build-up of fluid and a 'hot spot'. This can be detected by feeling the suspected part of the leg and then placing the hand on another part of the leg to see if it feels cooler by comparison. The horse will also let you know if the leg is tender by moving it away from your touch and maybe even being reluctant to have it touched at all. Sometimes a horse – maybe a racehorse or hunter – has naturally weak tendons and this requires specialist treatment.

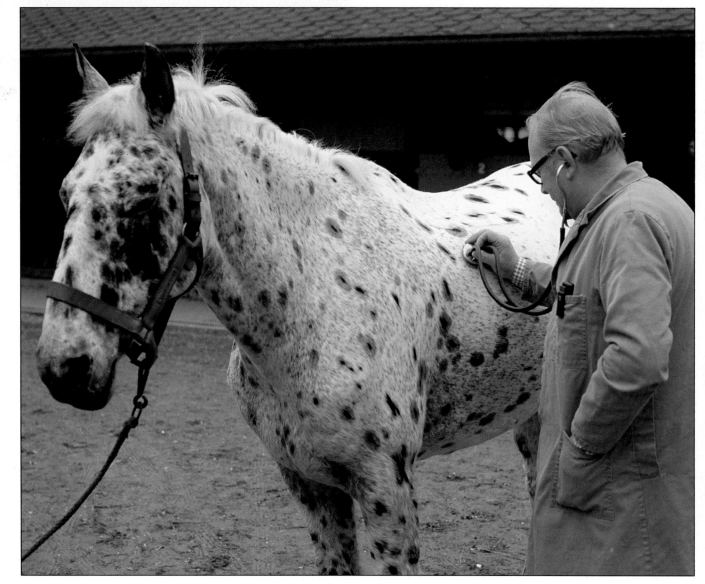

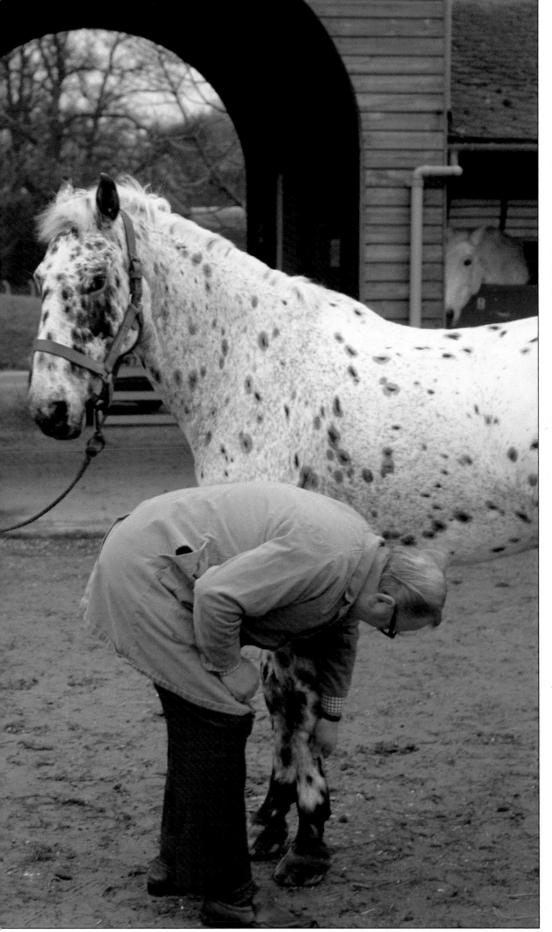

Above: As part of the routine inspection, your veterinarian will put the horse through its paces to see how it handles and how it moves, and at the same time pick up on any additional faults such as lameness. An honest owner should be perfectly willing for such an examination to take place. During this assessment you will be not only able to see if the horse has been schooled to the level the owner says, but also check how it responds to people and to different situations such as being led, being ridden (especially among road traffic) and its reaction to water. However, not all such veterinary inspections prove to be successful in diagnosing a possible vice, as these may occur only several days later. These problems can include wind sucking and crib-biting, where the horse gulps in air, sometimes with a post or other object between its teeth. This is usually a result of boredom and will interfere with the horse's digestion. The only cure is to keep the horse as occupied as possible. When buying or considering buying a horse or pony for a youngster, do allow for the child to grow quite a bit over the next year or so – or be prepared to buy another horse before very long. Also find out why the previous owner wants to sell the horse.

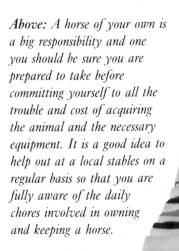

Above: *A horse of your own is a big responsibility and one you should be sure you are prepared to take before committing yourself to all the trouble and cost of acquiring the animal and the necessary equipment. It is a good idea to help out at a local stables on a regular basis so that you are fully aware of the daily chores involved in owning and keeping a horse.*

Left: *The amount of tack available today can be daunting, but only the most dedicated enthusiast would invest in the full range of clothing and equipment. Most horse owners are able to manage with the absolute essentials which, if you always look after them properly, should last for many years.*

Right: *Once you have decided on a horse, and you have both become acquainted, you will begin to know each other's capabilities. You may choose to compete with your horse in local events, where you can both display your individual and team skills. Before jumping, make sure that you have both had some sort of advance training, because it is not as simple as it looks.*

Right: The Welsh pony is one of the most popular breeds throughout the world and includes four different types generally referred to as sections. The first section, A, is the Welsh mountain pony that stands just under 12 hands high; then there is the section B, or Merlin, an elegant show pony that stands up to 13.2 hands. Section C, the Cob type Welsh pony, also stands up to 13.2 hands, and makes an ideal strong trekking pony. Section D is the Welsh cob; a strong muscular horse that is capable of carrying a heavy rider over a long distance. It stands anything from 13.2 to 15.1 hands high.

Left: Many people's first experience of riding a horse takes place not in the familiarity of their home country, but away on holiday. This may be in the exciting and exotic surroundings of a foreign vacation with a skilled instructor in tow to offer advice and encouragement. Riding along a beautiful beach with the sun on your back and your well-groomed horse splashing through the shallows can be a relaxing way to take a little exercise. When you get back home, the enthusiasm may linger but the day-to-day reality of owning a horse might seem a little more like hard work. If your enthusiasm is restricted to weekend or vacation riding, there are plenty of riding holidays available, from trekking in the mountains to 'Wild West' weekends for rodeo enthusiasts. There is usually no need to have a mount of your own - although you can take your horse if you have one and the distances make this practical.

Above: There is no point in spending a great deal of money on a top-class mount that shows excellent potential as a dressage horse or eventer, when all you really want is a good-natured horse with plenty of stamina for leisurely rides through the open country. You will not need all those smart competing clothes either - but sensible protective clothing is a must, especially if you are riding alone or over rough terrain. In particular, a hard hat or helmet is essential.

Tack and stabling

Before you bring your new horse or pony home you must make two major decisions: where to stable it and what type of tack to buy. If your horse is loose in a field without any shelter in the form of hedges or trees, it will need a stable to wander in and out of whenever it needs to take cover. Stabling need not be a major expense and will go a long way towards preventing unwanted illnesses, costly remedies and veterinary bills. The size of the shelter will depend on the size of your horse or pony. The most popular shelters are built of wood, with a sloping roof to keep off the rain and help prevent condensation building up on the inside and dripping onto the horse. Sheet metal or galvanized steel are alternative materials. The stable should have a slightly sloping hard floor made of concrete or similar material to stop water from running in and creating a pool. Alternatively, the floor should be slightly higher than the ground outside so that there is a small step up into the stable.

Efficient draftproofing is vital, as most of the finer breeds are more susceptible to the cold than outdoor horses. During cold spells, rugs will also help overcome this problem. If several horses are kept together, say at a livery or racing stables, the requirements are somewhat different. Each horse should be housed separately, but if the front of their shelter overhangs the door the horses can see one another over the stable door but not from the inside. This prevents them from biting and causing each other unnecessary injury and allows them to look out without getting wet.

The tack you choose, i.e. saddles, bridles and other equipment, depends on the type of activity you enjoy. If you use your horse for leisurely cross-country riding, then you only need basic riding equipment. Close-fitting clothes are probably best, but provided you feel comfortable and the horse is not shy of loose flowing materials, ordinary outdoor clothing will do just as well. Unless you ride without a saddle, your footwear should depend on the size of the stirrups. Narrow-sided boots that allow the foot to move freely in and out of the stirrups are the safest and make mounting and dismounting easier. Should you have a fall, you can slip your feet out of the stirrups and avoid being dragged along behind the horse. You will need a range of equipment to keep both horse and stable tidy - not just brushes, combs and cloths for grooming, but also a light barrow for cleaning out the stable, pitchforks, shovels, brooms and zinc or vulcanized rubber buckets. These items should be heavy-duty but not unwieldy. A sack for carrying straw is useful, and a hosepipe, preferably with an adjustable nozzle, is essential for washing down.

Above: When several horses are stabled together, you can economize on bedding by shaking out the straw and keeping the clean material to use again.

Left: This Arab stallion is being led with a very thin lightweight bridle that shows off more of the horse's head. Avoid injuring the eyes or teeth when fitting bridles.

Right: Neatly rugged up for warmth and with its legs bandaged to avoid injury during transit, this horse is bound for a show. There are many different kinds of horse rug on the market today and choosing the right one can be confusing. There are heavy-duty outdoor waterproof rugs, thermal rugs and lighter weight thin rugs for summer - all available in a wide range of colors. It is important to make sure that a rug fits correctly. If it is too tight it may rub the horse, especially over the withers and at the shoulder, causing discomfort.

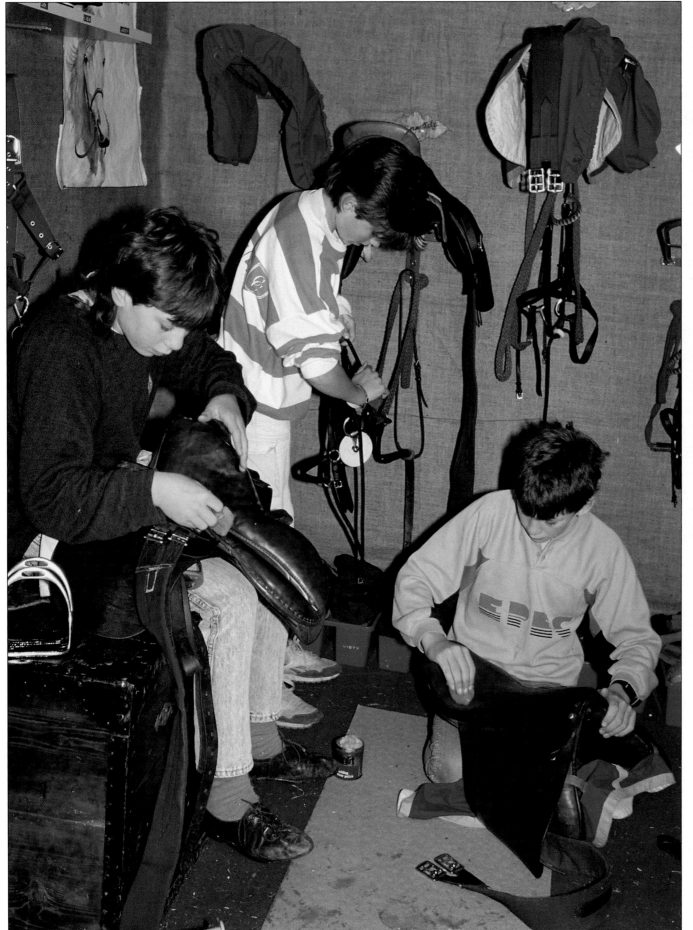

Left: Special shows and displays require a tremendous amount of preparation, particularly when a whole team of riders is involved. Each piece of tack must be sorted out so that all the items match and then each piece is carefully cleaned and polished. Brightly colored clothing, bridles and girth bands lend an extra sparkle to the event.

Above and left: Transporting your horse - or horses - also needs careful consideration. A small, lightweight horse box, such as the one pictured left, can transport two horses at a time, yet is easily towed by almost any size car fitted with a suitable towbar. The much larger, more elaborate towing trailer might include living accommodation for the rider too, including a kitchen and shower. Always check that your vehicle is in good working order and conforms to the highway regulations in the area where you are traveling. Make sure everything is ready before you load your horse or horses. Try to make the ride as smooth as possible and provide your horse with protective clothing to prevent injury.

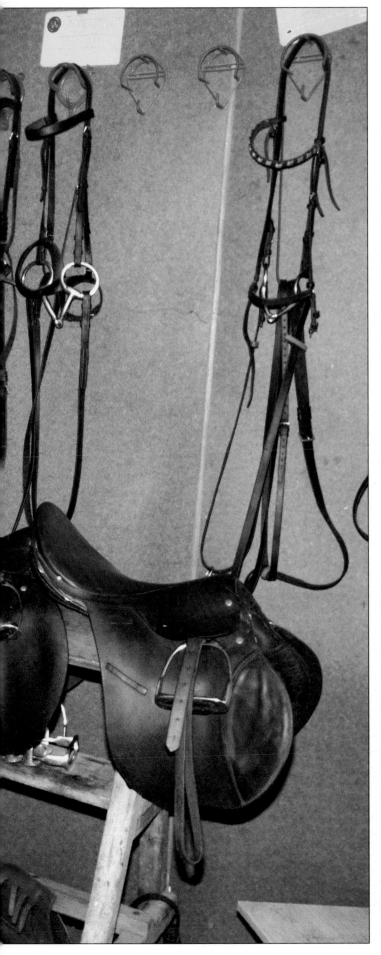

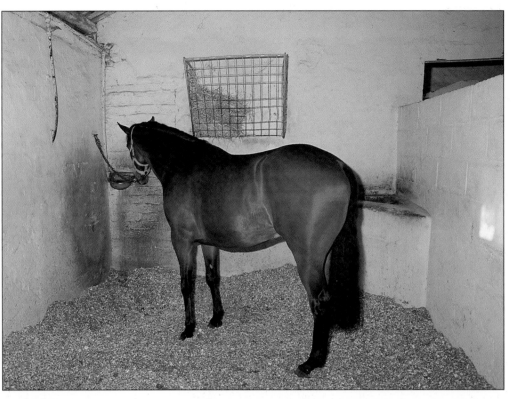

Left: Make sure that the stable is kept in good order, with all the pieces of tack laid out so that everyone knows just where to pick up the right equipment. This prevents the risk of confusing your tack with that of another rider.

Above: A clean, tidy and safe stable. The hay rack is high up so the horse's legs cannot get tangled up with it, the water and food troughs are separate, and the walls are whitewashed. The horse is standing on a bed of shavings.

Below: Buying tack can be expensive and it is important to keep it in good condition. It is a good idea to clean all the pieces at the same time, to check them over for damage and replace any that are worn out or potentially dangerous.

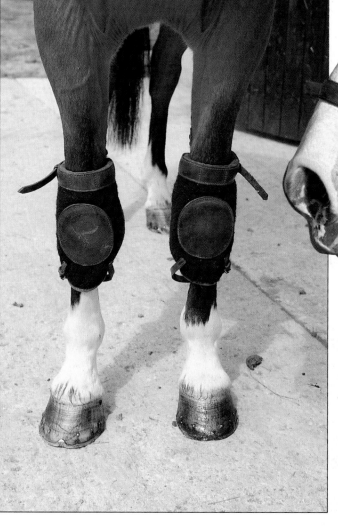

Below: *A very common type of bit and bridle with dropped noseband and snaffle bit. The bit works by putting pressure on the corners of the horse's mouth when the reins are pulled. The dropped noseband goes under the chin of the horse, thus helping to* keep the bit in place. It also prevents the horse from opening its mouth to allow the tongue to pass over the top of the bit. The standard noseband serves to improve the horse's appearance when bridled, although if fitted tightly enough, it may discourage the horse from opening its mouth. Other types of noseband provide more or less control.

Above left: *When you sell a horse you might wish to emphasize some of its finer features by using smart pieces of tack, such as this small showing saddle. It helps to give the impression that the horse has a good, well-shaped back and sides and does not have any significant skin disorders. This saddle is also easier to put on and take off.*

Left: *Some horses are susceptible to damaging their knees, particularly when they are out jumping .One way of overcoming this problem is to use knee boots. These are made of leather and padded on the inside for extra protection. Other boots are designed to protect the rear of the leg. Protective plastic traveling boots are easy to secure.*

Above: This rider is wearing novice dress for a dressage event. If you are seriously considering taking up eventing, you will need to think about the time involved, the cost of traveling and the effort of transporting your horse to different venues, as well as the special clothing and tack that you and your horse will both need to look and feel the part.

Right: Medium dress for a dressage competition. If you are not sufficiently smartly turned out for an event – particularly dressage – you could lose points for untidy presentation or even be disqualified. Check out the rules and regulations beforehand from the organizers to avoid disappointment. The horse's saddle or bridle should be coordinated to suit your mount. Also be sure to check that nothing is loosely fitted and hanging freely, such as buckles and straps.

Left: A high-class stable in the USA. Even the outside of the building is covered in so that both the stable blocks, which are conveniently opposite each other, are sheltered. This is an ideal arrangement, particularly during wet or stormy weather, enabling you to groom your horse in the dry. This extra covered space may be useful for storing pieces of riding equipment and horse feedstuffs.

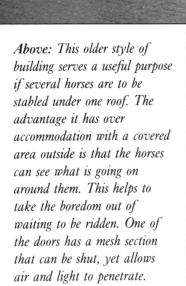

Above: This older style of building serves a useful purpose if several horses are to be stabled under one roof. The advantage it has over accommodation with a covered area outside is that the horses can see what is going on around them. This helps to take the boredom out of waiting to be ridden. One of the doors has a mesh section that can be shut, yet allows air and light to penetrate.

Left: Some horses are really intelligent escape artists. Having once found out by chance how to open a catch or handle on the stable door and let themselves out, they persist in trying to do so again and again. This kick bolt is fixed out of reach of the horse at the bottom of the door and is designed to overcome the problem of repeated escapes and provide peace of mind for the anxious owner.

Caring for your horse

To keep your horse in a good, healthy-looking condition, you must keep it clean, and this means grooming it regularly. Every animal needs some grooming, particularly domesticated creatures, otherwise they soon begin to harbor dirt, disease and parasites that can make them seriously ill. In the wild, horses groom one another to a certain extent and also roll around in the dust and mud to help reduce the number of lice and blood-sucking insects. Carrying out regular grooming and preventative medical care gives you the chance to keep an eye on what is happening to your animal, both externally and internally. For example, some forms of fly, such as the bot fly, lay their eggs on the horse's coat or legs and are then taken into the horse's stomach when it licks itself. When the eggs hatch out they live inside the intestine in the form of worms or larvae. They live off the horse's food supply, robbing it of essential vitamins and minerals, until they are ready to pass through the system, hatch into flies and begin the cycle all over again. Unless the animal is wormed to counteract such parasites, it will not look in good condition or be truly healthy.

If your horse is harboring lice, it will usually roll about and rub itself in a bid to relieve the irritation, and its coat will become dull, sore and scaly. There are many proprietary powders and solutions that you can apply to prevent these insects from attacking, so there is no need for your horse to be subjected to discomfort.

Providing your horse has never been frightened or startled (spooked) while it is being groomed, it will enjoy being rubbed down and appreciate being cooled off in hot weather. Groom your horse every time you return from a ride and have removed its tack. This will help it to settle down and relax its muscles. It also enables you to see whether it has picked up anything on its feet or sustained any cuts on the body and legs, particularly if you have been jumping obstacles. It is also a good idea to go over your horse on the morning before a ride, because injuries may not be immediately apparent. If you should find any lameness or swelling, it is best not to ride the horse, as this will only make the condition worse. Treat the injury if you can, but always call on the services of a veterinarian if you are in any doubt or if the injury does not heal quickly. Brush and pull the mane and tail to keep them growing straight and evenly layered. Once it has become bushy near the dock, the tail can be difficult to reshape. Tail bandages may help to keep it in place.

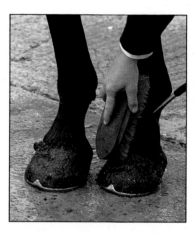

Above: Always clean the feet of the horse thoroughly before and after it has been ridden. Take the time to do this job properly because it will prevent the build up of impacted mud. A hosepipe is useful for washing off heavy dirt.

Right: A good overall wash every now and then will benefit your horse as it will get rid of all those minute particles of grime that a brush cannot shift. It is a good idea for someone else to hold and calm the horse as you work on it.

Left: Gently wiping the eyes and face with a wet sponge will not only refresh the horse, but also clean away any unwanted dirt and sweat. Always hold the head to prevent the horse turning round as you clean it, and be gentle - the muzzle is a very sensitive area.

Above: Plaiting the tail is difficult and takes time and patience. Not all horses will stay still long enough and may kick. A stable door between you may be the answer.

Below: A well-plaited tail is the finishing touch for the most smartly groomed horse. Once finished, make sure that the horse does not rub against anything or it will get spoiled.

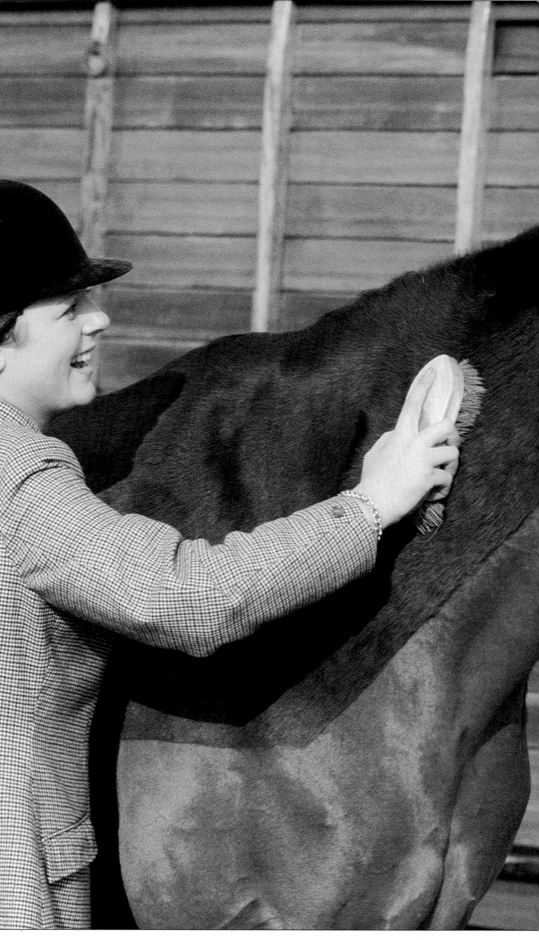

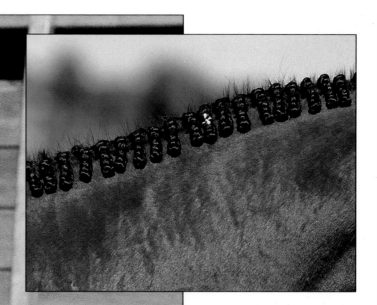

Above: There is more than one recognized way to plait a horse's mane. This is known as US plaits - a row of well-spaced, tight braids that look particularly formal. The technique is not easy: the short hairs have to be woven in as you go along, without the plaits slipping or becoming too loose. Done properly, this will help to show off a strong neck.

Left: Brushing over with a dandy brush helps to stimulate the muscles as well as keeping the coat clean and healthy. Brushing strokes should be kept as smooth as possible and always with the flow of the hair growth. Some horses find the dandy brush tickles them too much and become jumpy, particularly when tackling the more sensitive underside areas.

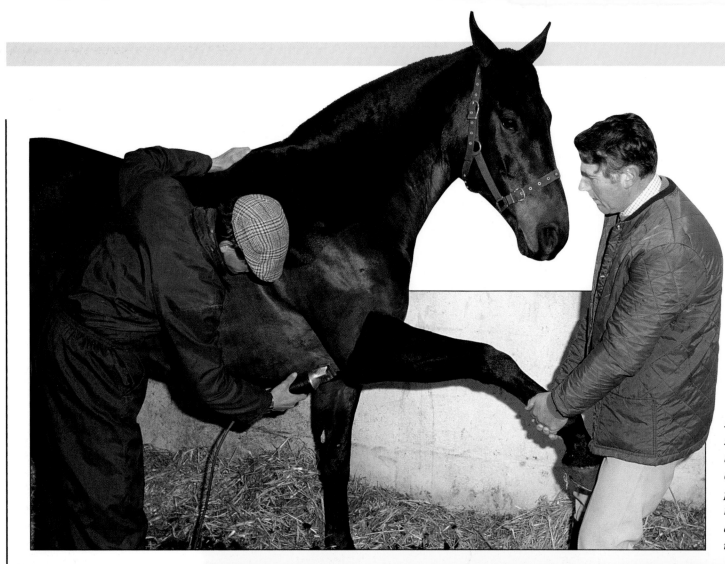

Left: Not all horses enjoy being clipped and may offer some resistance. To help discourage the animal from backing off, hold up one of its front legs. This throws the horse off balance should it try to kick out. Also, as shown here, it helps to have an assistant when clipping under the legs. There are several types of clipping style, such as hunter clip, trace clip, blanket clip or clipped right out. Clipping the coat short is primarily designed to prevent the horse sweating too much and to make a muddy coat much easier to clean.

Right: This home-made corner manger makes a wholly suitable feeding trough. It has a non-porous bottom to prevent the feed from losing any of its goodness, as some feeds are soaked to make them more digestible. Positioning the manger in the corner of the stable means it is out of the way; the horse can still feed easily but you are less likely to bang yourself on it. Importantly, there are no sharp edges on which the horse can damage itself. A ring in the wall close by is useful for tethering the horse near the manger while it is eating and is also handy for keeping it in one place while it is being groomed. Make sure that your horse has cleaned all of the previous feed out of the trough before renewing. Never simply 'top up', as the old feed underneath will become stale and possibly toxic.

Left: One of the biggest problems with bulky foodstuffs is how and where to store them. The place where you keep your feeding ingredients should be dry yet well ventilated to keep them fresh, easily accessible but protected from rodents. Each horse should be given the right amount of food in accordance with its weight and the amount of physical work or exercise it has. For example, a horse that does not do any work soon becomes overweight and out of condition, whereas a hardworking horse will burn off more energy and thus need a higher calorie intake.

Overleaf: In many parts of the world, wintertime is understandably the hardest time of year for outdoor horses and everything possible should be done to ensure that they survive it as comfortably as possible. Here the feeder provided for them is combined to take both hay and grain, hay on the top rack and the grain underneath. Although horses will scratch at the frozen ground and seek out grass, hay should be available at all times should they need it. Some form of simple shelter where the horses can take cover is a good idea; this need only be a small shed where they can come and go freely.

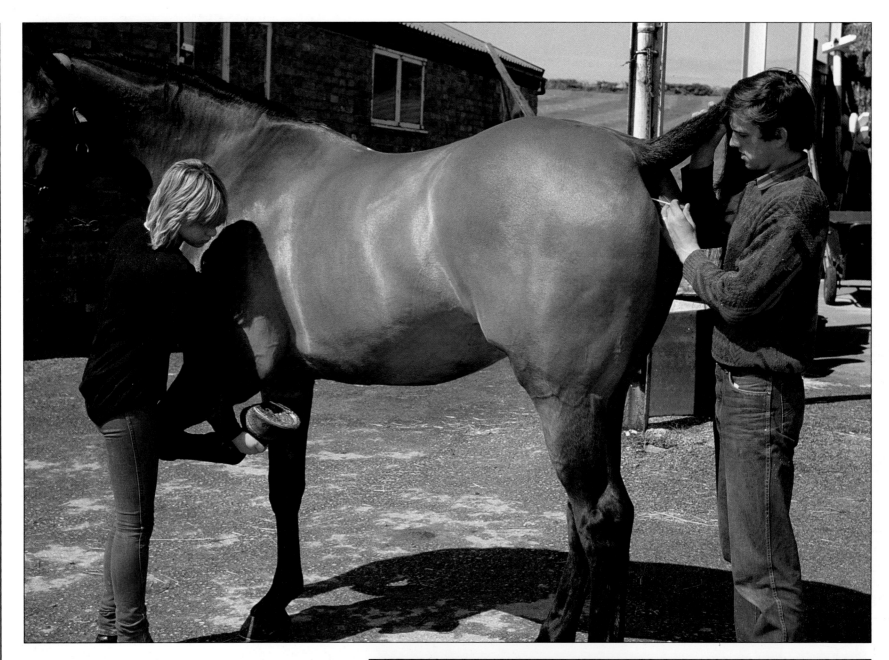

Above: Should your horse show any signs of illness, such as heavy breathing, heaving flanks, excessive thirst or the base of the ears becoming warm, when no exercise has been taken, its temperature should be taken. The normal is 100.5–101°F (38.1–38.4°C). You can do it yourself if you have the correct thermometer and someone to hold the horse's front legs to prevent it kicking. Sweating followed by quickened breathing and general restlessness is usually a sign that the horse is in pain.

Right: Checking the horse's tendons and ligaments is important because an animal with any weakness or damage must not be worked without protection and requires daily treatment if the condition is not to worsen. If the tendons are naturally weak, the horse must only be worked in bandages. Standing in cold water, a cold compress and rubbing with embrocation can ease any swelling, as will rest. The ligaments at the back of the cannon bone are the ones most likely to be injured.

Below: *If your horse is living outdoors and it is in poor condition, it is a good idea to check on its teeth to see whether or not they are growing properly. If they are not level, it becomes difficult or even impossible for the horse to grind grass with the molar teeth, and it begins to suffer nutritionally. Also, the teeth* *can become broken and the sharp edges can result in a sore mouth. This could make it difficult for the horse to eat. Uneven growth and any sharp edges can easily be eradicated by means of a rasp or file. The process is quite painless and should usually be carried out at least once a year. Seek expert help for these tasks.*

Right: *Sore eyes are caused by flies and are most likely to occur in summer. You will notice that the eyes become sore and watery with a discharge. Bathe them with cold weak tea, a solution of potassium permanganate or boracic acid, then apply an eye ointment as recommended by your veterinarian.*

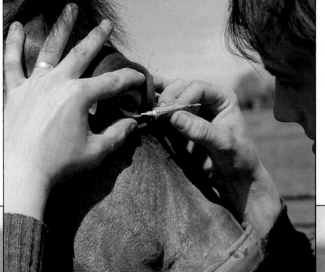

Schooling and exercise

A horse is like any other animal that is to be trained: it needs to learn right from wrong at the earliest possible age if later training problems are to be avoided. In the case of a foal, this means as soon as it is out and about. Like all creatures, a horse is much harder to teach when it is older and any bad habits are more difficult to break. Use a firm but calm voice to get your message across to the animal without frightening it. Never startle your horse out of frustration or temper, as this will only cause the animal to distrust you and probably do the opposite of what you want. Gradually you will earn its confidence; a horse knows instinctively when the person it is with is in the least bit nervous and will react by becoming totally stubborn and unmanageable or frightened and skittish. In either case, such behavior can be very dangerous and may result in someone being injured. Be firm but calm in your commands and totally consistent: reprimand the horse in a sharp tone as soon as it has done something wrong so that it knows exactly what the mistake was and when it was made. A firm loud 'no' is usually sufficient. At the same time, be sure to acknowledge and pet the horse when it does right, for as it gains confidence in you, it will gradually begin to obey the more specific instructions and demands you make on it.

Do not expect too much of your horse after only a short period of schooling. It takes a great deal of time and patience to reach an understanding, although there is no doubt that some horses are much quicker to learn than others. During the early stages of instruction the horse should learn to understand and act on the simplest commands, such as 'easy boy' (or girl); 'whoaa'; 'move over' and 'walk on'. It will soon get used to your tone of voice. Tackle one command at a time and repeat it patiently until the lesson is learnt. There is no point in pressing on with more advanced training until all the basic stages have been completed.

Much of what you teach your horse will involve simple forms of exercise that will benefit both horse and rider, so look on your schooling sessions as doing you both a lot of good. Fresh air and exercise are essential if the horse is to develop healthy lungs, heart and muscles, so introduce a structured routine of walking, running and possibly jumping. Even if you do not have permanent access to a field or paddock, be sure to exercise your horse regularly in a yard, a nearby park or in local woodland. If you do not have time to exercise the horse yourself every day, arrange for someone else to do it. Enthusiasts without a horse of their own are often keen to help out in return for a chance to ride. Remember that a horse that is looked after by one person for any length of time soon becomes devoted to them and will find it difficult to respond to another person's commands or calls. It will need plenty of time to adjust to a new owner or even to being looked after by someone new.

Left: If it is not practical or convenient to take your horse out for its regular exercise, you may decide to use lunging reins, but you will need plenty of space.

Right: Early morning exercise starts the day on the right footing and gives the horses at this riding stable a chance to loosen up as they gallop out together.

Below: Some horses need strict and patient schooling to reach their full potential. Here, a high-stepping Tennessee Walking horse is being put through its paces.

Right: You must expect to encounter many different kinds of obstacles while out riding in the country, and a closed gate is almost certain to be one of them. Providing the gate is hinged well and opens freely, there should be no need to dismount to open it. Closing the gate after you is just as important. However, it takes a lot of practice to achieve this type of maneuvering, as not all gates have the same fixings.

Below: Sometimes the only way that you can travel without going over neighboring land is by road. It is very important to be sure that your animal can cope with sudden noises, such as fast cars or motorbikes. Never take out a horse that you cannot trust absolutely on a road, especially if it shows a fear of vehicles while still in the yard or paddock. This could end in a serious accident to you, your horse or other road users.

Right: Circus horses are taught many different techniques, including kneeling, rearing up on their hindlegs and bowing to an audience, but it takes a long time to train them to perform the necessary maneuvers. To encourage the horses, tasty tidbits or morsels of food are offered as an incentive during training. In the past, the horses were often subjected to harsh, often cruel training methods. Today, however, trainers tend to concentrate on the animal's instinctive behavior and inclinations. Here, the horse is encouraged to draw its head right back by offering it a tidbit and this results in the animal making the required gesture.

Right: It takes hours of practice each day to produce the peak performance that this Olympic champion is capable of. The rider must time every movement and instruction precisely to the second. As the horse learns the different motions in dressage, the ultimate aim is to create an impression of a single fluid movement. To be successful, the horse must be physically perfect and totally obedient.

Left: Not all horses take to the water very well and some never get used to it at all, even though they may perform excellently in all other respects. This can be very frustrating for the rider, particularly in competitive events, as most courses usually incorporate some form of water feature that must be successfully negotiated. Three-day events even involve jumping into the water, sometimes over rails to make it even more difficult.

Right: Training a horse to jump correctly is a slow and careful process requiring much patience and skill on the part of the rider. If the horse is commanded to jump too soon, it will often fall short of the objective, with the animal becoming tangled up or crashing on top of the poles. Leaving the instruction to jump until it is too late means the horse will simply plow aimlessly through the barrier.

Right: Horses are natural jumpers and can jump surprisingly high when faced with obstacles such a gate, hedge or formal jump. Begin training by laying poles on the ground for the horse to walk over. Later on, try creating a makeshift jump, using old oil drums with poles placed on the top. Leave the poles unsecured in case the horse should catch them with its hooves.

Right: Practising the dressage routine at home is usually far easier than doing it in front of a crowd of eager spectators and a panel of judges. Sometimes the horse will work well in its own environment, but is quite reluctant to do so when under pressure in a competitive situation.

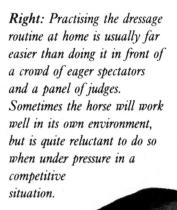

Above: Racehorses need to be exercised thoroughly every morning. Some stable owners employ several jockeys and grooms to carry out this daily routine. Here they are exercising the horses before the day's big race.

Left: This horse walking pen is designed to exercise several horses at the same time – a useful schooling device for large stables. The horses can walk freely in a circle around the ring, all attached to a central pole.

Right: Steeplechasing requires a horse to run fast and jump without hesitation. The back is straight, the legs are bent and the head is allowed to stretch forward naturally. The rider sits tucked close to the horse.

Left: *Sharp cornering around obstacles such as this barrel helps to teach the horse the correct maneuver. The rider tugs on the reins according to the direction in which he wishes the horse to turn: a pull to the right means make a righthand turn and vice-versa.*

Below: *Before jumping low obstacles, the horse should be accustomed to walking over poles on the ground. Encourage it to move in a straight line by placing two vertical objects at the ends of the 'course'.*

Right: *Long reins can be used to exercise both mounted and unmounted horses. They are simply an extension of the normal control reins used for riding. The horse can be controlled by the master walking some distance behind it. The animal will soon learn to obey a variety of controls and signals, such as being made to go on from behind, and also to turn left or right. The young Lippizaner horses at the Spanish Riding School spend much of their training in long reins of this type.*

Right: Some people think that their horse is the only one that needs to be superfit to be able to compete against other horses in any kind of event, let alone a strenuous one. However, as any equestrian that has had competition experience will tell you, the rider has to be reasonably fit as well, especially for some of the more rigorous riding that requires plenty of strength. This is especially true of hard, gruelling long-distance rides over rough terrain, as here.

Business and pleasure

Many people throughout the world choose to keep a horse for the combined purpose of business and pleasure. This is especially true in remote hill areas and inhospitable spots, where vehicles are impractical or simply not available. There are some societies that deliberately choose not to own motor vehicles and are quite happy to carry on just as their forefathers did for hundreds of years before. Certain tribesmen live so close to their horse that it hardly leaves their side throughout the whole of its life - much like the relationship that can develop between a man and a working dog that also becomes a close friend. This relationship between man and horse leads to a greater understanding of each other. In the past, farmers would have used their horse for pulling the plow or cart, for going to the local inn, visiting neighbors and traveling to market and annual fairs and festivals. It is heartening to know that such traditions continue in certain parts of the world, not just as a matter of choice but because they still represent a practical way of life.

In less remote regions, horses are often bred and kept for pleasure rather than for work, and some of the old working breeds are becoming rarer. Yet this trend is changing as man becomes more aware of the growing ecological problems caused by the motor car. Working farms and early industrial museums offer a glimpse of how life used to be and this may help to preserve some of the old breeds.

The horse is probably the most versatile animal that has ever existed, and has been bred and trained for many purposes. As we have already seen, horses are involved all over the world in a huge range of leisure activities, often in hard and inhospitable conditions, from hot dry deserts to arenas of ice. Wagon racing and dray pulling, reminiscent of the old Roman chariot racing, are becoming increasingly popular and exciting for competitors and spectators alike. The preparation that goes into such events can involve a good deal of time and money, particularly if you have a team of eight or more horses, and if it were not for the enjoyment of the sport there would not be so much interest. Some winners can take home a considerable amount of prize money, but the true horseman or woman will tell you that they join in simply for the love and excitement of competing. Other people just like owning a horse and riding it regularly. They do not become involved with horse spectacles and competitive trials, but are happy to enjoy leisurely rides in the countryside and woodlands, and experience the satisfying companionship of a horse for many years.

Above: In many parts of the world, pack horses are a familiar sight, carrying loads of firewood and other cargo. It is important that loads are distributed evenly on either side of the animal to prevent falls on narrow pathways.

Left: A ranch hand in Nevada. In the USA, horses are still the most efficient means of herding and driving the wild horses and controlling the cattle on the dusty plains. A horse must have stamina and intelligence for this work.

Right: The Hillsborough mounted police stage an impressive display for the public. A coordinated demonstration of their equestrian skills is a good public relations exercise and proves that police work has its more agreeable side.

Right: Sometimes it is necessary to tether your horse outdoors to prevent it straying. This horse in Guatemala has been tethered close to the shoreline so that its owner can load his catch of fish onto it without having to walk very far. The time that a horse is left tied up and unsupervised should be kept to a minimum, because the weather is not always predictable. Heavy rain, freezing winds or burning hot sun will soon cause an unprotected horse to suffer. The rope should be of good quality, and must never be tied directly around the horse's neck. This could lead to a fatal accident if the horse becomes entangled and unable to free itself. Always use a head collar and attach the rope to this instead.

Left: *Ranchers in Texas and other rough country terrains use horses to cross their land as they inspect stock and boundary fences. On horseback they are able to get close to herds of grazing animals without disturbing them. Riding in the saddle across the open countryside, the rancher is more in touch with nature.*

Below: *As well as for work, a horse and cart such as this one is ideal for making short local trips at a reasonable speed. A simple cart could also be modified by covering it over and adding doors and a window so that it becomes a mobile home. This used to be a popular method of transport with traveling circus people.*

Left: *A working horse in Russia pulling a load of hay in addition to the weight of three adults on a home-made four-wheeled cart. The main load rests on the wheels and body of the cart, which takes the weight off the shafts. It is steered by a swivel through the front axle that pivots from side to side whenever the horse is commanded to go left or right. The harness fits behind the horse's legs so that it cannot stretch them out too far. If this happened the horse would risk hitting its legs against the front of the cart, quite possibly sustaining an injury. The horse must have strong legs if it is to pull such heavy loads about for any length of time.*

Left: Sleigh riding is a popular pursuit in certain snow- and ice-covered resorts, such as this one in St. Moritz in Switzerland. Apart from transporting tourists around, sleighs are useful for carrying goods and supplies to the hotels and chalets dotted about on the hillside resorts, where motor vehicles find it difficult or even impossible to reach.

Below: A mounted police display in Calgary, Canada. Many countries have a mounted police force, which is used for ceremonial occasions, controlling riots or patrolling the parks and towns. The horses must be specially trained not to rear or bolt when faced with noisy traffic, pressing crowds or unexpected hazards.

Above: On important ceremonial occasions, teams of highly trained horses take their part in the role of pulling the royal coaches. These coaches are very intricate and many date back hundreds of years to the days before motor engines.

Before the horses are allowed to pull the coaches, they will have undergone a great deal of training to make sure that nothing goes wrong with such a precious cargo. It is vital that they do not bolt at any sudden noises or disturbances.

Below: City police find horses particularly useful when confronting violent incidents. The horses undergo rigorous training to teach them to cope in difficult conditions and the officers must be able to handle a horse in hostile situations.

Right: Working horses in Nevada driving cattle. They play a vital role in the farmhand's life, each man looking after his own horse. It is much more practical to equip the men with a horse than with a conventional vehicle, as it easier to reach stray cattle in awkward places on horseback. Wherever a herd of cattle can roam, a horse and rider can surely follow.

Below: Once the herds of cattle have been rounded up from the surrounding open countryside, they are driven into the corral, where they can be sorted into different groups as required. Even here the rider stays on his horse to part the individual animals and thus avoids being stampeded or trodden on by the feet of these heavy cattle.

Right: The Shire horse at work. It is one of the most popular heavy breeds for farm work. Until the beginning of the 20th century, Shire horses were a familiar sight among UK farming communities, where nearly every farm had its own team of horses. Today they are more likely to be seen at working rural museums, and it is always worth going to a demonstration to admire the strength and control of these impressive horses. See too how the farmworkers display their driving skills as they operate traditional implements, such as this horse-drawn drill. These old skills are much more difficult to acquire than they look and require far greater experience and expertise than handling modern machines. They also rely on a strong mutual understanding between man and beast.

Right: The art of keeping a team of horses working together as shown here looks fairly easy. It is however quite the opposite, for each individual horse has its own temperament and may respond to the master's voice differently. It is he alone that calls to them, at the same time guiding them with the reins and whip to keep all four on form. They must act according to the circumstances and position of the carriage at any time. This type of competition is still a popular sport that goes back centuries to Roman times, when chariot races took place in and around the arenas.

Above: Battling it out on the corner, these six contenders are all trying to reach the winning post first. It is virtually impossible for them to pass one another, particularly when they are so close together, as here, and it takes a good deal of experience and precise timing to accomplish the move.

Left: The Icelandic pony is a very strong muscular animal, capable of carrying a good deal of weight over long distances. Its coblike build and long flowing mane, tail and forelock give the horse a certain youthful and slightly wild look, making it a popular leisure riding pony.

Right: These two Ardennais horses are finding it very easy to pull a heavy cart around the arena - a simple task compared to what they would once have been doing every day on the farm, when the day began at dawn and finished at dusk. Although they are not worked to the same extent today, because their role has been superseded by modern equipment and technology, these heavy horse breeds have devoted owners who are determined to keep the breeds going. Without their dedication, we may not have the opportunity to see these fine horses in action at local and international shows.

Entertainment for all

Ever since man first tamed the horse, he has enjoyed showing off his skill at handling it and competing in tests of speed and dexterity. The invention of the wheel brought a new dimension to horse riding in the form of chariot racing - a sport still enjoyed today by the cowboys who hurtle chuck wagons and a team of horses around the course at their local rodeo. Right across the world there is a vast number of exciting horse-based sports and spectaculars, some of which date back centuries and are virtually unchanged, while others are relatively new. Some sports involve the owners in huge costs and the horses themselves may be almost priceless. Others are simple homely affairs in which anyone with a horse can compete. However, one thing is certain: these events are frequently as much fun for the spectator as for the rider or driver.

A horse spectacular may be as formal as the disciplined military maneuvers performed by the mighty white Lippizaners from the Spanish Riding School of Vienna, which can kick, crouch or rear in a special sequence of medieval battle actions. In contrast, consider the pomp and glitter of the circus horse, trained to gallop around a small ring with several acrobats balanced on its back at the same time. The rodeo offers quite another horse spectacular: wild bronco riding, for example, and the more skilled steer wrestling. Every country has its own specialty, from high

speed ice racing in Switzerland, known as skijoring, to horseback archery in Japan. Many of these sports and displays are based on ancient military traditions from the days when the cavalry was the mainstay of the army and horses were specially bred to cope with battlefield conditions. It is surprising just how many popular sports involve horses, from steeplechasing (racing over fences and hurdles) and flat racing to ball sports, such as fast and furious polo or el pato - a skilled form of mounted basketball. In the USSR there are up to 40 different horse-based sports, including wrestling, fencing and spear-throwing. But perhaps the most thrilling sport of all is endurance riding, a competitive ride over long distances and the roughest terrain - a real test of stamina in which the horses are frequently checked for injury and withdrawn if necessary. You may prefer not just to watch but to take part and even if the event is not quite as exciting as those described above, the experience of riding a horse and maybe competing for a rosette is satisfying enough. The tiniest tots can try their skills in the children's classes at local events, while older riders might prefer the rough and tumble of cross country or the discipline of show jumping, smartly turned out and aiming for perfection. Not all riding activities are a test of the competitive spirit; a leisurely ride through the woods or a trekking holiday in rather wilder landscapes can be equally enjoyable. Given the broad scope and many opportunities offered by the different types of horses and activities, there is truly something for everyone, from the television spectator at home watching the racing, to the handicapped child who is given a wonderful chance to enjoy fresh air and exercise on the back of a horse.

Above: Games such as fancy dress races, dropping balls into a bucket from horseback and this obstacle race can be fun for horse and rider and a chance to show off their coordination and skills.

Far left: If you love riding and enjoy a bit of an adventure, what could be more enjoyable than a trekking expedition in the Rockies? For safety, make sure you have expert supervision.

Right: Chuck wagon racing is fast and often dangerous. Wagons are drawn by a team of four horses, seen here in action at the famous Calgary Stampede, one of the most popular rodeo events.

Left: Pony clubs are great fun and an excellent way to improve your riding skills. Under the instruction of qualified and experienced riders, young enthusiasts learn a wide range of maneuvers and handling tips at regular meets and annual camp holidays. Members receive routine schooling and also practical advice on correct care for their horse and stable management. These pony club meetings also provide fun and games for the participants, teaching them that not everything to do with the horse world has to be taken seriously. Games might include anything from fancy dress to relay and obstacle races and bobbing for apples.

Below: Both the horse and rider pictured here are well turned out for an important show. If you hope to compete in such events, your dress and the horses's tack must be correct and adjusted before the judging begins, since any defects are noted and deducted from the overall score. In some cases, participants may even be disqualified from a particular event for, say, simply failing to wear a pair of gloves. Thoroughly groom your horse before the event to create a good impression. Cleaning the tack is equally important, as any dirty or out-of-condition item will soon stand out from the rest, especially when it is put on a clean pony or horse.

Left: Horse trials are always anticipated with great pleasure and some trepidation. They provide an opportunity for competitors to show off their riding skills at a range of events, and are also social occasions when horses and their owners can meet and make friends and exchange news – and this includes parents when the event is aimed at younger riders, as here. Trials are not only a chance to show off your horse and general riding ability, but also more specific skills, such as jumping and maneuvering. Most horse trials include some jumps, even in the children's classes, and some of the small ponies are capable of clearing quite high fences. Although fences for younger riders are usually a lot smaller than professional jumps, young riders wishing to exercise their jumping skills must be sure that both they and their horses are fit and confident.

Right: The benefits and opportunities that riding can offer to disabled people have been recognized for a long time, and there are many riding centers that are specially adapted to the needs of those confined to a wheelchair or handicapped in other ways. Getting to know all about riding horses and taking the responsibility for grooming them helps to provide both physical and mental stimulation. It is surprising how mobile and active even a fairly seriously disabled person can become once mounted on four fast legs, but none of this experience would be possible without the unselfish assistance offered by the helpers, many of whom donate their valuable time on a voluntary basis.

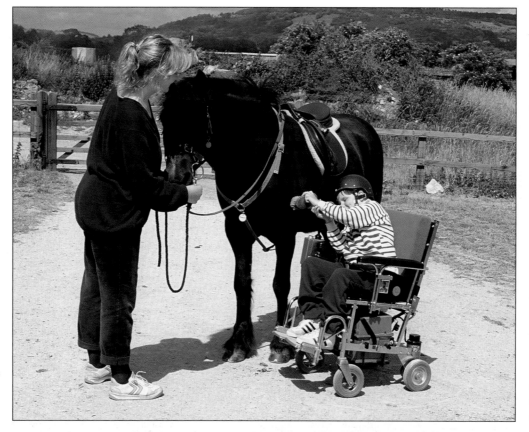

Right: Trekking makes a marvellous horseback holiday for experienced and novice riders. Usually you can take your own horse or hire one from the trek center. A qualified leader takes you out on trail, camping in cabins or chalets along the way. Traditional trekking ponies are small but strong.

Below: Winter sports resorts can offer a lot more besides skiing and tobogganing. Horses are very much a part of scenes such as this, being one of the easiest means of getting about. These children are enjoying an invigorating pony ride through the crisp snow. Later on, their parents might decide to take a traditional horse-drawn sleigh ride into town.

Left: *Horse racing has been a popular and structured sport, with a strict set of rules, since the Ancient Greeks. It takes place all over the world, on grass, sand, snow and ice. The horses must be highly bred and spirited to compete successfully and the English Thoroughbred - or racehorse - has been developed over the last 250 years to meet these demands.*

Right: *Jumping calls for a good deal of concentration from both the horse and rider if the fence is to be cleared successfully. The timing has to be precise, especially on a high fence jump: too soon and you end up hitting the middle of it, possibly hurting the horse; jump too short and the horse's hindquarters may bump into it.*

Below: *Members of the Cadre Noir from the Cavalry School at Saumur put their powerful sauteurs, or jumpers, through their paces, which include dressage, show jumping and military techniques.*

Below: *Roping a live animal whilst galloping on a horse close behind is by no means an easy task. The timing and movements have to be spot on in order to swing the lasso over the top of the beast's head and neck successfully.*

Right: *Although the famous wild horses of America's wide plains are almost extinct, Mustang or Bronco riding is still a popular part of the exciting annual rodeos held in the USA, Canada, Australia and New Zealand.*

Left: *The game of polo is one of the oldest sports in the world. It originated in Persia and was discovered by the Crusaders. The ponies must be top class - fast and intelligent, yet robust and steel-nerved. The game is exciting but exhausting, and each player needs two or three ponies so the animals can rest after each playing period. For this reason, polo has a reputation for being an expensive sport for the players. Far from being a gentlemanly pastime, it is rough, tough and dangerous. The rider needs a strong empathy with his horse and great skill to hit the wooden ball with his long-handled mallet. Horse and rider require long, vigorous training in order to compete successfully.*

Index

Page numbers in **bold** indicate major references, including accompanying photographs. Page numbers in *italics* indicate captions to other illustrations. Less important text entries are shown in normal type.

Picture credits

The publishers wish to thank Bob Langrish for supplying the majority of the photographs for this book. All are © Bob Langrish.

Other photographs have been supplied by C. M. Dixon as follows: Title page, 10(TR, BR), 11(BL, BR).

Right: Once you have learned how to handle your horse or pony with confidence, you can try jumping small fences and obstacles. With practice, you may graduate to proper showjumping, an exciting and popular sport for participants and spectators alike. The stakes are high and the margin for error is extremely narrow when every vital second and each inch can make the difference between winning and losing a prestigious event. A good showjumping horse should be well built, with long sloping shoulders, well-angled legs and an easy fluid movement.

monica Prince

monica Prince

MONICA PRINCE

you are
so cool!